CHAPTER 1

THE PATH TO REAL ESTATE OPPORTUNITIES

When it comes to embarking on your real estate investment journey, the first puzzle piece is discovering the right properties to invest in. The question arises: how do you uncover those sellers who are brimming with motivation? What's the significance of these motivated sellers anyway? In the ever-shifting realm of real estate, motivations can change like the wind. Some individuals are eager to part with their properties, while others experience shifts in perspective. The key is to identify motivated sellers, individuals with a keen interest in swiftly and efficiently transferring their property.

But why does finding such sellers matter? Well, motivated sellers are inclined to sidestep prolonged negotiations and cumbersome paperwork. They're focused on a quick and seamless sale, and this presents a golden opportunity for you. Engaging with motivated sellers can lead you to properties priced below market value, a strategic move that can boost your financial returns.

For those with aspirations of thriving in real estate investment, the task isn't just about locating sellers ready to sell.

It's about pinpointing sellers who are primed to sell at the right price or according to terms that align with your strategy. If you encounter a seller unwilling to align with your vision, don't hesitate to pivot and explore other options. The real estate realm is a tapestry woven with opportunities, and there's no shortage of paths to explore.

Your objective in the real estate investment game is to maximize returns. If a seller's asking price veers too far from your financial goals, it could erode your potential profits. That's why identifying the right sellers holds the key to unlocking your investment success. Imagine this scenario: a property with immense potential catches your eye, but the seller's reluctance to expedite the process dampens the prospects. This could lead to unforeseen costs like taxes and utility bills eating into your budget. And if the deal collapses, it's an ordeal you'd rather avoid.

But fret not! The journey to discovering motivated sellers isn't a complex equation. In this chapter, we're about to unveil a strategy that can have you connecting with motivated sellers in less than a month. Say goodbye to waiting endlessly for your inaugural investment. Motivated sellers are spread across the landscape, and with a little effort on your part, you can unveil their locations.

Always remember: no matter how promising a property seems, a disinterested seller could shatter your plans.

Now, let's dive into the tactics for locating motivated sellers and securing your first property:

The Power of Lists: A treasure trove of information lies within lists that spotlight motivated sellers. Individuals relocating, changing jobs, or grappling with mortgage payments are often poised for a swift sale. Their urgency is your advantage. Lists of these sellers can be found at places like your local tax office or online.

Crafting Persuasive Outreach: Armed with these lists, it's time to reach out to potential sellers. But here's the catch: you need to convince them to choose you as the buyer. Your message must strike a professional, clear, and enticing tone. Reach out via letters, phone calls, or face-to-face meetings. Paint a picture of how their life could transform by selling to you.

Embrace Direct Mail: Believe it or not, old-school mail still packs a punch. The humble yellow letter is a case in point. Personal and effective, these letters can be used to gauge a seller's interest in selling or seeking a buyer.

Appeal to Emotions: Elevate your direct mail by evoking emotions. Share anecdotes from your real estate journey or highlight the potential of their property. Forge a connection that makes selling to you an appealing choice.

Realistic Expectations: Not every letter will trigger a response. On average, direct mail boasts a 5% response rate. Yet, even without a reply, your message may leave an impression.

Harness Online Platforms: Digital platforms are your ally. Craigslist, We Buy Houses, and Facebook offer avenues to connect with motivated sellers bypassing traditional routes. Moreover, aging listings might offer opportunities as their prices drop.

Timing is Everything: Listings lingering for 30 days tend to witness price reductions. It's a strategic waiting game. If you act swiftly when the time is right, you might just snag an exceptional deal.

Be Prepared to Move On: Not every opportunity is a match made in heaven. If a seller isn't onboard with your terms, it's wise to gracefully bow out. A wealth of alternatives awaits those who remain flexible.

Unearth Creativity: When standard methods yield lackluster results, embrace ingenuity. Contemplate your ideal seller profile and tailor your approach. While trial and error may be part of the process, persistence pays off.

Cherish Relationships: Exceptional customer service remains a linchpin. Forge bonds with potential sellers, even if they're not ready to sell right away. These connections could yield valuable insights or opportunities in the future.

The journey to real estate triumphs commences with the discovery of motivated sellers.

The road might be winding, but armed with the right techniques and unwavering commitment, you're poised to unearth hidden gems that can pave the way for financial prosperity.

This chapter is your guidebook, leading you to those elusive sellers who hold the keys to your real estate triumphs.

CHAPTER 2

REAL ESTATE SUCCESS THROUGH DILIGENT MANEUVERS

Embarking on the intricate journey of real estate investment demands more than just excitement – it necessitates strategic navigation. Enter the world of due diligence, where meticulous research and careful preparation shape the trajectory of your investments. Whether you're a seasoned investor or a newcomer exploring the market, the significance of due diligence is profound.

A Foundation of Integrity and Profitability: At its core, due diligence serves as the bedrock of ethical and lawful business practices. It ensures that commitments are honored when entering agreements. However, in the realm of real estate, due diligence extends further, encompassing rigorous research before sealing a deal. This process can be the catalyst that transforms a potential venture into a thriving success or a cautionary tale of losses.

Balancing Risk and Reward: Imagine standing at a crossroads where each decision influences the balance between risk and reward. Due diligence acts as your compass in this intricate terrain. One pivotal aspect involves accurately gauging the potential costs of property rehabilitation. Yet, its scope reaches beyond numbers, embracing the meticulous completion of forms, adhering to tax obligations, understanding code regulations, and settling utility fees.

It's a choreography of precise steps that collaboratively create a smooth and legally sound journey.

Navigating Legal Terrain: The legal aspect of due diligence is paramount. This phase provides investors and buyers a golden opportunity to scrutinize a property's condition and ownership status before committing. This period typically spans between 7 and 30 days, allowing the liberty to withdraw from an agreement if unexpected issues arise. Unearthing concealed structural flaws or problematic lease agreements during this window can avert significant setbacks.

Capitalizing on the Due Diligence Window: The due diligence phase isn't a mere countdown – it's an active interval for exploration and validation of your investment. Collaborate with professionals such as inspectors, contractors, lenders, and real estate attorneys to gauge the property's potential. Dive into potential rehabilitation costs, envisioning the investment's return. This is a moment for comprehensive research, meticulous calculations, and the foundation for a prosperous endeavor.

Insurance: A Guardian Amidst Uncertainty: In the intricate world of real estate, where variables abound, insurance emerges as a sentinel against unforeseen challenges. It's not just a line item in your financial plan; it's peace of mind. Builder's risk insurance, tailored for property flipping, serves as a shield against construction-related risks. Meanwhile, vacant property insurance offers a buffer against vandalism, fire, theft, or natural disasters during extended projects.

Exploring the Labyrinth of Liens: Liens, often dreaded by homeowners, can serve as a treasure trove for investors.

The intricate dance of unpaid property taxes, utility bills, or mortgage loans can lead to properties hitting the auction block. For astute investors, this presents an opportunity. However, as a novice, remember that genuine due diligence involves understanding a property's background and liabilities before leaping into an enticing deal.

Unveiling Property Value through Appraisals: Appraisals hold the key to unveiling a property's true value. During due diligence, this tool becomes a potent asset. The appraisal value isn't merely a monetary figure; it's a guiding star for negotiations and insights into potential returns. Appraisals empower you to make informed decisions, ensuring your investment aligns with your financial objectives.

Thorough Inspection: Beyond Surface Impressions: Appearances can be deceptive, but the foundation reveals the truth. Rigorous inspections during due diligence unearth hidden structural issues, pest infestations, or code violations that could undermine your investment. Collaborate with property inspectors to unveil the property's secrets, steering you away from expensive surprises post-purchase.

Untangling the Threads of Title History: The history of property ownership conceals crucial information you can't afford to overlook. In this meticulous phase, ensure the ownership record is impeccable, free of contradictions or liens that might jeopardize your rights. Errors in this area could result in financial losses or legal entanglements best sidestepped.

Navigating HOA Dynamics: For properties within

homeowners associations (HOAs), familiarity with their dynamics is essential. Monthly fees and levies contribute to communal upkeep, directly impacting your profitability. Due diligence entails understanding these financial obligations, ensuring no unforeseen costs eat into your returns.

Deciphering Zoning Regulations: Zoning regulations are a critical piece of the puzzle, influencing property function and usage. Neglecting zoning laws can lead to unexpected complications, such as difficulty securing insurance or loans. During due diligence, uncover the property's zoning status, aligning it with your investment vision to avoid stumbling on unforeseen roadblocks.

Illuminating Lease Agreements: Amid the dance of due diligence, focus your attention on lease agreements and associated paperwork. Engage a real estate attorney to ensure these documents are airtight, safeguarding your interests throughout the investment journey. Complexity abounds here, and professional guidance can avert costly misunderstandings.

A Symphony of Prudent Decisions: As you weave through these layers of due diligence, envision a symphony of decisions, each note contributing to your harmonious real estate investment journey. Mistakes born from haste or negligence can shatter the melody.

To aid your orchestration, we unveil the mistakes you must avoid:

- Avoiding the Abyss of Wrong Investment: Failing in due diligence can lead to purchasing the wrong property, a grim scenario where unforeseen issues surface after the investment. Diligence ensures your investment is based on comprehensive knowledge, not just a façade.
- Target Market Tune-Up: Real estate investment is akin to a stage performance. Without understanding your

target market's desires and dreams, your property remains an overlooked extra rather than the leading act. Tailoring your property to their aspirations ignites the spotlight on your investment.

- Cultivating Connections: Building a network is akin to nurturing a garden – it requires tending and patience. Ignoring networking means limiting opportunities. Forge relationships with professionals and peers, enabling advice, insights, and unforeseen opportunities to flow.
- Buyer List Brilliance: Harness the power of a buyer list – a cadre of interested buyers eagerly awaiting your offerings. However, creating the list is just the opening act. Nurture these connections, ensuring they remain engaged and interested throughout your investment journey.
- Contractor Chronicles: Cutting corners with contractors can lead to subpar outcomes, undermining your property's value. Due diligence extends to researching and selecting competent, reliable contractors who uphold your investment's potential.
- Balancing Budgets: In the symphony of investment, budgets form the rhythmic foundation. Accurate budgeting ensures you don't miss a beat. Allocate resources wisely to avoid draining profits or falling short on necessary expenses.

Wholesaling: A Unique Investment Choreography: In the world of real estate, two distinct rhythms emerge – the rhythmic dance of house flipping and the unique choreography of wholesaling. Wholesaling is a swift ballet that doesn't demand extensive renovations; instead, it focuses on leveraging distressed properties for profit. This technique involves contracting a property at a discounted rate and swiftly transferring the contract to another buyer at a slightly higher price.

Advantages and Disadvantages of Wholesaling:

- Advantages: Wholesaling offers a quicker route to profit compared to house flipping, requiring less financial investment and reduced hands-on effort. It's an entry point for novice investors to gain experience, confidence, and capital before pursuing larger endeavors.

-       Disadvantages: While wholesaling minimizes financial investment, its returns are also lower compared to house flipping. The process demands precision timing, coordination, and networking prowess. In the absence of reliable buyers, your investment could unravel.

Closing the Curtain on Deals: As the curtain draws on your due diligence process, ensure you have all elements in place for a grand finale.

Secure financing, review contracts, and collaborate closely with legal advisors. Embrace due diligence as your guiding star, illuminating each step of your real estate investment journey.

Crafting Your Unique Symphony of Success: Remember, every property you invest in is a note in the larger symphony of your investment portfolio. Each diligence-driven decision is a stroke of your conductor's baton, guiding your orchestra toward a crescendo of accomplishment. Harness the power of due diligence, blend it with your unique insights, and let your real estate symphony resonate with prosperity.

CHAPTER 3

THE ART OF ESTIMATING REHAB COSTS

Welcome to the realm of estimating rehab costs in the world of real estate investment. Picture this as piecing together a puzzle, where each fragment represents a financial aspect, and assembling it reveals the financial landscape of your venture.

Decoding After Repair Value (ARV): Imagine the ARV as the ultimate worth of your investment once all enhancements are in place. It's akin to foreseeing a masterpiece as you envision the value of a house after all the transformations. Buy a property at $200,000 and allocate $50,000 for improvements, and your ARV blossoms to $250,000. To flourish, you must sell beyond $250,000.

Crafting a Strategic Budget: Visualize your budget as a blueprint guiding your endeavor. Think of it as steering clear of extravagant spending while constructing a dwelling. Overshooting 70% of the

ARV is a no-go. Say repairs tally at $50,000, and your target sale is $270,000 – a $20,000 profit. Stray from the budget, say, buying at $220,000, and red ink might flow.

Selecting Repair Endeavors: Consider this as handpicking repairs that align with your vision. There are three repair categories to sort:

> Simple Upgrades (Cosmetic Repairs): These are modest tasks, like painting and fixing floors. Initial costs might be higher, but completion is faster.

> Middle Ground (Moderate Repairs): A tad complex, like bathroom refurbishments. They consume more time and funds but promise enhanced returns.

> Ambitious Projects (Extensive Repairs): The elaborate tasks, such as structural fixes or additions. For seasoned investors, these beckon, but costs – both time and money – run high.

Clock Management: Navigating Carrying Costs: Think of this like orchestrating the rhythm of your project. Carrying costs are the background hum – taxes, interest rates while you own. Like harmonizing music, align these costs for the right tempo, ensuring you're on track.

Tools of the Trade: Leveraging Helpful Resources: Imagine resources as tools in your toolbox. Investigate material and service expenses. Seek contractor estimates for clarity. Platforms like Fixr, HomeAdvisor, and Homewyse provide insights. Wander hardware stores to acquaint yourself with prices.

These tools empower informed decisions.

Learning from Aces: Seeking Expert Guidance: Envision gleaning wisdom from seasoned experts. Connect with veteran investors or contractors – a mentorship of sorts. It's akin to seeking advice from those who've done it before. Dodge common pitfalls, embrace sagacious choices.

Adapting to Market Fluctuations: Embracing Change: Consider this adapting to the market's shifting tempo. Imagine tuning your musical instrument to match evolving melodies. Factors like taxes, material availability, warrant adaptability. Sync with market dynamics.

Reaping the Harvest: Transforming Efforts into Profit: Picture it – the crescendo of your investment symphony – reaping profit. It's akin to the pinnacle note in a composition. Post meticulous planning and endeavor, your asset is primed for sale. The zenith of your investment voyage.

Evading Missteps: Learning from Blunders: This mirrors avoiding discordant notes in a musical piece. Watch for these pitfalls:

Cultivate Patience: Rushing akin to offbeat tunes. Allowing time for growth is vital.

Check the Foundations: Secure footing is paramount. Analogous to music grounded in harmony, solid groundwork anchors your investment.

Master Research: Delve into details. Ponder costs and expectations. Failing to research could derail your investment melody.

Ride Market Waves: Imagine surfing market surges. Like

rhythm changes, market dynamics shift. Navigating these changes is pivotal.

Tap Expertise: Don't shy from seeking advice. Just as a mentor guides a musician, seasoned investors or contractors can steer your journey.

An Odyssey, Not a Sonata: A Constant Learning Curve: Remember, estimating rehab costs is an odyssey. Visualize it as mastering a musical instrument – each property a fresh composition. With practice, you refine, akin to a musician's artistry.
It's not a one-act play but a continuous voyage, polishing skills for financial triumph.

CHAPTER 4

THE ART OF SKILLFUL NEGOTIATION

Welcome to the world of negotiation, where the art of deal-making takes center stage. Think of it as a symphony of strategies, a delicate balance of understanding and influence that shapes successful outcomes.

Getting Prepared: Setting the Scene for Negotiation

Imagine yourself as a director before a play. Just like they ensure everything is in place before the curtain rises, you need to set the groundwork. This is your opportunity to spot potential advantages or pitfalls that could make all the difference.

Harnessing Persuasion: Crafting Compelling Arguments

Picture negotiation as the art of persuasion. It's about more than just numbers; it's about psychology and influence. Ever wondered why prices often end in 99 cents? That's the power of psychological nudging. You'll be using similar techniques to sway discussions your way.

Storytelling Magic: Elevating Communication for Impact

Envision negotiation as storytelling. Instead of waiting for the other party to see the value, you're painting the picture. Take them on a journey through the property's potential. Help them visualize cherished moments in that dining room or the joys of a blooming garden. Building this emotional connection makes your offer irresistible.

Discovering Common Ground: Uncovering Needs

Imagine negotiation as solving a puzzle. It's about fitting together the pieces so both sides walk away satisfied. Dive into what sellers and buyers truly seek. Sellers might need a quick sale, while buyers dream of long-term investments. With these insights, you can sculpt an agreement that fulfills everyone's desires.

Strategic Play: Mastering Control

Think of negotiation as a strategic game. Sometimes, letting the other side feel in charge can be your secret weapon. It's like a strategic move on a chessboard, directing the flow to your advantage. Staying composed and guiding the conversation can lead you to success.

Balancing Power: Leveraging Strength

Imagine negotiation as a seesaw. The side with more leverage has the upper hand. Know your strengths and theirs, uncovering the pressure points. This positions you for powerful negotiation.

When you're not desperate to close, you're more likely to sway things your way.

Confidence Catalyst: Projecting Assurance

Think of negotiation as a job interview. Confidence is your suit and tie. When you show you're not desperate, you're in a stronger position to negotiate the terms you want. Confidence empowers you to stand firm and lead the conversation.

Persuasive Tactics: Artful Communication

Envision negotiation as a friendly conversation. It's about gentle influence, not force. Utilize techniques like echoing key points, giving something before taking, and subtly guiding thoughts. These artful methods can steer the negotiation toward your intended destination.

Adapting Approach: Tailoring Strategies

Think of negotiation as a toolkit with versatile tools. Adjust your tactics for each scenario, like a tailor crafting a suit. If wholesaling, tap into emotions. For home buying, meld assertiveness with empathy. Tailoring your approach to the situation is your key to triumph.

Timing Wisely: Syncing with Market Flow

Picture negotiation as a dance with market rhythms. Timing is your partner. Patience can lead to superior deals, but linger too long, and the music might fade. Stay attuned to market patterns, allowing you to choreograph your moves perfectly.

Knowledge Power: The Negotiator's Arsenal

Envision negotiation as a puzzle solved with information. Understand property values, market tides, and financial boundaries. Empowered with knowledge, you're equipped to navigate negotiations effectively.

Mutual Success: Crafting Collaborative Solutions

Imagine negotiation as building a bridge, ensuring everyone crosses unscathed.

It's not about outmaneuvering, but about finding solutions that suit all. Transparency and integrity foster trust. A fair deal now can forge fruitful partnerships later.

Mastery Journey: Evolving Skills

Think of negotiation as an ever-evolving craft. Like refining a skill or mastering an instrument, practice is key.
Every negotiation refines your technique, hones your emotional intelligence, and polishes your deal-making prowess. A journey where learning never ends.

CHAPTER 5

NAVIGATING THE REAL ESTATE DEAL MAZE

Welcome to the world where real estate dreams become tangible reality. In this chapter, we'll take you by the hand and guide you through the labyrinth of real estate transactions. It's a journey filled with twists, turns, and the excitement of sealing the perfect deal.

Deciphering the Deal Dynamics: How Purchase Agreements Unfold

Imagine purchase agreements as the master key to real estate deals. These documents are the glue that holds every detail together. They outline the rules of engagement, providing a roadmap for both buyers and sellers. Think of it as a compass that points toward successful transactions.

Blueprints of Success: Anatomy of Purchase Agreements

Think of a purchase agreement as a tailor-made suit. It's meticulously stitched to fit the unique contours of each deal. Within its pages lie the details that shape the destiny of the transaction. Just as a blueprint is essential for constructing a building, a purchase agreement is essential for constructing a deal.

A Closer Look: What Purchase Agreements Contain

Imagine opening a treasure chest filled with essential elements. Purchase agreements are rich with specifics that ensure clarity and transparency. From property descriptions to earnest payments, everything is neatly organized. It's like a puzzle coming together, piece by piece.

Show of Commitment: The Power of Earnest Payments

Think of earnest payments as a symbolic handshake. It's a way to say, "I'm serious about this deal." This monetary gesture showcases commitment and good faith. It's as if both parties are locking arms, ready to embark on a mutually beneficial journey.

Crunching Numbers: Taxes and Interest Rates Unveiled

Imagine stepping into a financial laboratory where equations are solved. Taxes and interest rates are the scientific variables of real estate. Understanding them is like deciphering an intricate code. It's a critical step to ensure financial clarity before sealing the deal.

Honesty Matters: The Truth About Interest Rates

Think of interest rates as the heartbeat of a deal. Transparency is key here. Concealing or inflating rates is like playing a tune with off-key notes. Openness ensures both sides are on the same page, creating a symphony of trust and fairness.

Contingencies: Preparing for the Unexpected

Imagine real estate as a chessboard, and contingencies are your strategic moves. They're provisions that act as safety nets against unexpected twists. From financing to inspections, they're contingency plans that allow both parties to make informed decisions.

Facing Reality: The World of Closing Costs

Imagine closing costs as the final curtain call of a theatrical performance. It's when the financial actors take their bow. These costs cover agent commissions, legal fees, and other expenses. Sellers shoulder a significant burden, ensuring a smooth transition of ownership.

Signatures and Seals: Binding the Agreement

Think of signatures as the seal of approval on a masterpiece. They validate the agreement, turning words into action. It's like signing an artist's canvas, signaling that the creation is complete and ready to be admired.

Countdown to Possession: The Closing Date

Imagine the closing date as the finish line of a marathon. It's the moment the keys to the kingdom are handed over. The property and funds exchange hands, like a baton in a relay race. This date is etched in anticipation, marking the culmination of the journey.

The Wholesaler's Role: A Different Kind of Dance

Think of a wholesaler as the conductor of a grand symphony. Their role orchestrates the harmonious connection between buyer and seller. They're like musical notes that bridge the gap, making deals possible even without direct ownership.

Passing the Torch: Responsibilities Transferred

Imagine a relay race, where the torch is passed from one runner to another. In real estate, the torch is the property's ownership. When you step into a contract, you're carrying that torch, ensuring its safe passage to a new owner.

Navigating the Legal Labyrinth: Paperwork's Necessity

Think of paperwork as a treasure map leading to the ultimate reward. It guides the way through legal waters. Certificates, payments, and bills must be squared away. It's like making sure all the keys are in place before unlocking the treasure chest.

Guided by Experts: The Role of Attorneys

Imagine attorneys as the Sherpas of the legal mountain. They're your guides, ensuring safe passage through tricky terrain. With their legal expertise, you're equipped to traverse the intricate pathways of real estate transactions.

Embracing Patience: The Art of Negotiation

Picture negotiation as a dance, where partners move in perfect rhythm. Rushing leads to stumbles, but patience ensures graceful steps. It's like painting a masterpiece—you layer colors thoughtfully, resulting in a work of art.

Safety Nets: The 72-Hour Rule

Imagine a safety net beneath a high-wire act. The 72-hour rule is just that—a safety net that prevents free falls. It provides a window of reflection, offering a chance to adjust without drastic consequences. It's like pausing a game to catch your breath.

Financial Preparedness: A Prerequisite for Success

Think of financial readiness as fuel for a journey. Before signing, ensure your resources are aligned.

For buyers, it's proving your purchasing power; for sellers, it's verifying a buyer's capability. It's like checking your wallet before stepping into a store.

Clear as Day: Understanding Inclusions

Imagine buying a car, only to realize the steering wheel isn't part of the deal. Clear communication is paramount. Specify what's included in the transaction, leaving no room for confusion. It's like describing the ingredients in a recipe for a perfect dish.

Integrity in Closure: Handshake of Honor

Think of closing a deal as a promise made in front of witnesses. It's a commitment upheld by integrity and trust. Like sealing a pact with a handshake, it signifies that both parties stand by their word.

Negotiation Mastery: The Art of the Deal

Imagine negotiation as a crafting table for masterpieces. Each deal is a unique creation, a fusion of tactics and strategy.
With practice, you become a maestro, orchestrating harmonious agreements that resonate with accomplishment.

CHAPTER 6

NAVIGATING THE TERRAIN OF FINDING EAGER CASH BUYERS

Having successfully identified promising properties and breathed new life into them, it's time to delve into the art of discovering enthusiastic cash buyers. Think of this process as a treasure hunt, where each buyer possesses a unique perspective and preference. Your role is to unravel their distinct desires, align them with the right property, and strike a deal that's mutually beneficial.

Deciphering Diverse Buyers: Tailoring Solutions to Individual Desires

Imagine yourself as a translator of aspirations, bridging the gap between buyers and properties. Just as people have their own inclinations for hobbies or flavors, buyers exhibit distinct inclinations. Some might seek coziness, while others prioritize space. Your task is to interpret their needs, match them with the ideal property, and orchestrate a harmonious agreement.

Crafting Symbiotic Deals: Balancing Buyer and Property Aspirations

Picture yourself as a conductor orchestrating a symphony of buyer and property interactions. The harmony lies in achieving equilibrium between what buyers seek and what properties offer.

In these balanced deals, you're composing a masterpiece that resonates with both sides.

The Magnetism of Cash Buyers: Fostering Confidence in Transactions

Imagine cash buyers as the reliable pillars of your real estate endeavors. They're akin to steadfast companions, always prepared to assist. With readily available funds, cash buyers expedite transactions and instill a sense of certainty in the process.

Dilemma of Speed vs. Profit: A Delicate Equilibrium

Envision a scale with speed on one side and profit on the other. Cash buyers tilt the balance toward swifter transactions, yet sometimes at a slight compromise on profit. This delicate decision involves weighing the advantages of quick sales against potential gains.

Wholesalers: Facilitators of Real Estate Interplay

Consider wholesalers as the architects of real estate matchmaking. They operate like bridge builders, uniting sellers and buyers. Wholesalers expedite transactions and streamline processes, akin to smooth operators who grease the wheels of the market.

Locating Wholesalers: The Pathway to Efficient Deals

Imagine wholesalers as guides leading you to hidden gems. They possess insights into locating exceptional properties and are equipped to introduce them to you. Collaborating with wholesalers offers an express route to securing favorable deals.

Leveraging Social Media: Engaging Buyers in Their Digital Haven

Think of social media as a bustling marketplace where you can flaunt your properties. It's akin to setting up a vibrant stall, showcasing images and videos of your properties to a vast audience. This dynamic platform enables you to connect with potential buyers who resonate with your offerings.

Property Staging: Elevating Properties to Their Full Potential

Visualize yourself as a curator of spaces, transforming properties into captivating exhibits. Staging is akin to painting a vivid portrait of a property's possibilities. By arranging furnishings and decor, you're enabling buyers to envision the property's potential, igniting their interest.

Consistency as Trust Foundation: Nurturing Credibility Through Quality

Imagine being renowned for consistency, like a dependable friend who always delivers. Ensuring every property meets a predefined standard is paramount. This consistent quality fosters trust and confidence among buyers, influencing their decisions.

Harnessing Referrals: Expanding Through Word-of-Mouth Connections

Think of referrals as whispers of recommendation that amplify over time. Delighting customers initiates a ripple effect, where satisfied buyers share their positive experiences. This network of trust spreads like wildfire, potentially leading to new connections and transactions.

Investing in Marketing: Amplifying Your Real Estate Voice

Picture marketing efforts as planting seeds that blossom into opportunities. Every advertisement and campaign serves as a beacon, drawing attention to your properties. The more you invest, the wider the net you cast, capturing the attention of potential buyers.

Building a Website: Your Online Citadel of Real Estate

Imagine your website as your digital headquarters. It's a virtual space where you display your properties, share insights, and communicate with potential buyers. Crafting an appealing website establishes your online presence and enhances your connection with buyers.

Harnessing Technology: Virtual Experiences and Beyond

Envision technology as a wizard's wand, conjuring immersive experiences for buyers. Virtual tours and interactive content allow buyers to explore properties remotely. This innovative approach kindles excitement and helps buyers visualize a property's latent potential.

Cracking the Code with Keywords: Elevating Your Online Visibility

Consider keywords as keys that unlock digital doors. By using relevant keywords on your website, you enhance your chances of being discovered by online searchers. Crafting strategic keyword content ensures your properties are showcased to the right audience.

When the pieces of the real estate puzzle finally fit together, it's time to dive into the intricate process of closing a deal.

This chapter acts as your compass through the maze of deal completion, unveiling strategies, techniques, and insights that can make this final step as smooth as silk.

Sealing the Deal Like a Pro: The Grand Finale

Think of deal closure as the crescendo of a symphony you've been composing. After sourcing sellers, calculating expenses, and enticing buyers, this is the moment your efforts culminate. This chapter guides you through the orchestration of a seamless deal closure.

Discovering Double-Closing: A Tactical Maneuver

Imagine having an ace up your sleeve when it comes to closing deals. Enter double-closing – a tactical approach where you execute two transactions simultaneously: purchasing the property and promptly reselling it. This strategic move can untangle complex situations and streamline the deal-closing process.

Transitioning to the Next Chapter: After the Applause

View deal closure as the final scene in one act, leading to the opening of the next. Once a deal is done, the spotlight shifts to your next move.

The transition may feel like navigating uncharted waters, but with strategic insights, you can transition seamlessly to your next real estate venture.

Six Key Steps to Successfully Seal the Deal

Envision a choreographed routine with six crucial steps, guiding you toward a triumphant deal closure:

Earnest Payment: Think of this as a down payment that signifies your commitment. It's a show of goodwill and often counts toward your final costs.

Inspection Odyssey: Imagine a thorough property inspection by professionals. This step ensures no hidden surprises and builds trust between parties.

Appraisal Exploration: Picture an expert assessing the property's value. It's crucial for both you and the lender to determine a fair price.

Shielding with Insurance: Think of insurance as a protective shield. Different policies safeguard you from unexpected twists and turns.

Final Walkthrough: Imagine a final rehearsal before the curtain call. This is your chance to ensure everything aligns with the agreement.

Final Act: Deal Closure: Picture the closing scene where signatures are exchanged, payments made, and ownership transferred.

Crafting Your Wholesaling Deal Closure: A 3-Step Symphony

Imagine a three-part composition for wholesaling deal closure:

Pre-Approval Prelude: Visualize securing approval before the main act. Pre-approval for a mortgage loan signals your readiness and eagerness to sellers.

Strategic Crescendo: Buy and Hold Ballet: Consider holding properties briefly to maximize profit potential. This strategy requires careful timing and market understanding.

Graceful Transition Encore: Envision moving seamlessly from one deal to the next. Reinvest profits, learn from missteps, and set goals to maintain momentum.

Epilogue: Your Ongoing Real Estate Sonata

Imagine standing at the finale of your real estate journey, having orchestrated successful deals and gained invaluable wisdom.
The lessons learned and strategies employed become your compass moving forward. Each completed deal serves as a stepping stone toward mastery.
By embracing adaptability, tackling challenges head-on, and applying your growing expertise, you are well on your way to becoming a seasoned real estate virtuoso.

Special Offer!

Loved Our Book? We're Excited To Give Back To Our Loyal Fans!

Get 5 Exclusive Digital Books For Free.

Email: infobookpub@Gmail.Com With The Subject As "Free Books"

www.ingramcontent.com/pod-product-compliance
Lightning Source LLC
Chambersburg PA
CBHW072227290526
45794CB00007B/2924